**DO NOT REMOVE
CARDS FROM POCKET**

MARIO LEMIEUX

WIZARD WITH A PUCK

BY BILL GUTMAN

MILLBROOK SPORTS WORLD

THE MILLBROOK PRESS

BROOKFIELD, CONNECTICUT

Published by The Millbrook Press
2 Old New Milford Road
Brookfield, CT 06804

Art Director: *Nancy Driscoll*
Design Management: *Italiano-Perla Design*

Photographs courtesy of:
Denny Cavanaugh: 4, 28, 30-31, 36, 39, 40, 43,
46; Federation Quebecoise de Hockey sur Glace:
7; Quebec Major Junior Hockey League: 9; *The
Montreal Gazette*: 11, 14; AP/Wide World Photos:
16, 18-19, 22, 27, 44; Bruce Bennett Studios:
3, 25; *The Pittsburgh Press*: 34.

Library of Congress Cataloging-in-Publication Data

Gutman, Bill.
Mario Lemieux : wizard with a puck / by Bill Gutman.
p. cm. — (Millbrook sports world)
Includes bibliographical references (p. 46) and index.
Summary: A biography of Mario Lemieux, detailing his
career as a hockey superstar with the Pittsburgh Penguins.
ISBN 1-56294-084-8 (lib. bdg.)
1. Lemieux, Mario, 1965- —Juvenile literature.
2. Hockey players—Canada—Biography—Juvenile literature.
3. Pittsburgh Penguins (Hockey team)—Juvenile literature.
I. Title. II. Series.
GV848.5.L46G88 1992
796.962'092—dc20
[B]
92-5003 CIP AC

MARIO LEMIEUX

On December 31, 1988, the Pittsburgh Penguins took to the ice to play the New Jersey Devils. The Penguins were led by center Mario Lemieux, already rated as one of the two best players in the National Hockey League. But on this night, Lemieux was in top form. His performance left the Devils reeling.

For openers, Lemieux had a hand in all eight Penguin scores. He came up with five goals and three assists for his second, eight-point night of the season. That tied a record set by Wayne Gretzky, the legendary player to whom Lemieux was most compared. But it was *how* Lemieux got his five goals that set him apart.

Whenever Mario Lemieux is on the ice, he threatens to dominate the game. Playing against the New Jersey Devils on New Year's Eve in 1988, Mario put on a show that will never be forgotten. He scored five goals and added three assists for eight points, becoming the first player in NHL history to score his five goals in five different ways.

There are five different ways to score a goal in the National Hockey League (NHL). Against the Devils, Lemieux became the first player ever to get one goal each way in the same game. He scored one when the two teams were at equal strength, five skaters on a side. He got another on a Pittsburgh power play. That means the Penguins had an extra skater on the ice.

His third score came with the Pens shorthanded. The Devils had the extra man. Then he scored a fourth goal on a rare penalty shot. A penalty shot has one player (in this case Lemieux) skating in on the goaltender alone for one free shot. Lemieux made it. His fifth and final goal came in the closing minutes. With the score 7-6, the Devils removed their goaltender. The idea behind this was to get an extra skater on the ice and try to tie the game. The strategy backfired when Lemieux knocked the puck into an empty net for his fifth goal of the night. He also iced the victory for his team.

Teammate Rob Brown marveled at Mario Lemieux that night. "Some of the things he did out there were amazing, even when he didn't score," Brown said. "He put the puck through his legs and made some dazzling twirls. It was a classic example of the best hockey player in the world."

After that game, many other people felt the same way Rob Brown did. At age 23, Mario Lemieux may well have become the best hockey player in the world.

THE HOCKEY LIFE

Ice hockey has always been Canada's national sport. For a long time, almost every player in the NHL was born in Canada. In recent years, more and more players have come from the United States. Now, many even come from

Europe and Russia. But most of the players are still born and raised in Canada. Boys in Canada often begin skating and playing hockey at an early age.

Mario Lemieux was born on October 5, 1965, in Montreal, Canada. His parents, Jean-Guy and Pierrette Lemieux, lived in a working-class section of the city. Jean-Guy was a construction worker, while Pierrette stayed at home to raise Mario and his two older brothers, Alain and Richard. Mario's family

Hockey often becomes a way of life for Canadian youngsters. Many boys learn to skate as soon as they can walk, and they practice the sport any chance they get. Mario Lemieux, like the youngsters here, played in leagues all the time while growing up.

was French Canadian. Like a lot of other people in Montreal, they spoke French, not English. Mario didn't learn to speak English well until he joined the Penguins.

What he did learn early on was ice skating. Hockey had always been very important to the people of Montreal. The NHL Montreal Canadiens had been the league's most dominant team since the 1920s. People in Montreal took great pride in the Canadiens. Almost every young boy dreamed of growing up and playing for the team. That's why most learned to skate almost as soon as they learned to walk.

There are stories all over Canada of children playing hockey from morning to night. They played anywhere they could find some ice. Some boys even left home when they were just 12 or 13 years old so that they could play against better players in other cities. Many families built skating rinks in their own backyards so their children could play hockey.

Jean-Guy Lemieux encouraged his hockey-playing children in a different way. He would pack his front hallway with snow from one wall to another. Somehow, the boys were able to skate on it and practice their hockey. Mario was the youngest, but he soon showed the most talent for the game.

Even at a young age, Mario had a strong desire to win. It didn't matter if it was cards, a game of Monopoly, or basement hockey. Whenever he played a game, he wanted to come out on top.

"If Mario lost, it would be as if a hurricane went through the basement," Jean-Guy Lemieux said.

Like many young Canadian boys, hockey quickly became the most important thing in the lives of the Lemieux brothers.

And that didn't change as the boys got older. It was hockey, hockey, and more hockey. Even school took second place.

Richard Lemieux, the oldest, gave the game up fairly early. But Alain was a good player. At 18 he joined a junior hockey club, called Laval, in Quebec, Canada. Mario followed him two years later in 1981 at the age of 16. By then there was little doubt that he was the best of the three brothers. As a 16-year-old, Mario quickly showed he could keep up with the older boys. His first year at Laval, he scored 30 goals and had 66 assists for 96 points. A year later, he jumped his total to 84 goals and 184 points. Suddenly, people began to notice him, both for his huge size and his talent. He was already becoming one of the better players in junior hockey. NHL scouts began to marvel at the sight of him. They saw how good he was at 17 and wondered how much better he could get.

With Laval, Mario became the best player in the junior hockey league. His third season there, 1983-1984, he scored 133 goals and had 149 assists for 282 points in just 70 games. His amazing scoring totals led to a host of awards, including the big one as Canadian Major Junior Player of the Year. He did this at the tender age of 18.

HERE COMES SUPER MARIO

Mario returned to the Laval club for the 1983-1984 season a year older and a much better player. As soon as the season started, everyone knew that he was now the best player in all of junior hockey. He could not be stopped. It was almost as if he scored each time he touched the puck.

There were times he used his skating and stickhandling ability to go around defensemen. Sometimes he just used his size and strength and went through them. He could do it with speed and he could do it with power. Either way, it was like a bunch of boys playing against a very big man.

The more Mario scored, the more attention he got. Defenders tried every way they could to stop him. They slashed and elbowed him, grabbing and hooking him with their sticks. Finally Mario decided to end the rough and dirty play.

It happened during a game at Laval when the other team assigned a "shadow" to guard him. A shadow is a defender who follows the star everywhere he goes on the ice, whether he has the puck or not. On this night, when the player shadowing him began slashing and hooking, Mario finally had enough. He dropped his stick and gloves . . . then hit the shadow with one punch! Mario got a penalty for fighting and had to leave the ice, but he succeeded in stopping the other player from playing dirty.

Mario had a very strong personality by this time. He still hated to lose

Mario was an outstanding hockey player at an early age. By the time he was playing with Laval in junior hockey, his bedroom at home had taken on the look of a real trophy room. Here, young Mario shows off some of the hardware he had already won. And it was only the beginning.

and played very hard every night. One night he not only scored seven points, but also ended up taking four penalties during the game. His coach didn't like the number of penalties. After the game he began yelling at Mario, calling him stupid for taking all those penalties. Mario whirled around and quickly pointed out that he had also scored seven points. But he didn't make a habit of talking back to his coach.

"One thing I hate is people screaming at me," Mario said. "If you want me to do something, talk to me. When someone screams at me to hurry up, I slow down."

There wasn't much slowing down during the 1983-1984 season, however. When it ended, Mario had an amazing 133 goals in just 70 games. He also had 149 assists for a total of 282 points. That comes out to an average of four points a game. He also had 29 goals and 23 assists in 14 playoff games. He won every award the league had.

By this time, every team in the NHL wanted him. He was already being called the next Wayne Gretzky. Gretzky, known as the Great One, was the best hockey player in the NHL, maybe the best ever. Gretzky, who had led the NHL in scoring at age 19, was 23 years old at the end of the 1983-1984 season. So Mario was being compared to a living legend, a player just coming into his prime.

Real superstars don't come along too often. They are special players who can sometimes carry an entire team to victory. Of course, in any team sport, it helps to have other good players on the team. No one person can do it alone.

Over the years there have been a handful of players thought to be this special. Maurice "Rocket" Richard was a great scorer for the Montreal Canadiens in the 1940s and 1950s. Bobby Hull, who played mostly in the 1960s and 1970s, was called the "Golden Jet" of the Chicago Black Hawks and made the slap shot a deadly weapon. He and Richard were the first of the 50-goal-per-year scorers.

Bobby Orr of the Boston Bruins was the first defenseman who could rush the puck up ice like a forward. He also played in the 1960s and 1970s and was one of the greatest skaters and stickhandlers in history.

Then, in the 1980s, along came Wayne Gretzky. The Great One simply rewrote the scoring record book. Coming into the 1984-1985 season, Gretzky had already won the league-scoring title five straight times. He had set single-season records of 92 goals, 125 assists, and 212 points. And in 1983-1984, his team, the Edmonton Oilers, had won the Stanley Cup, the trophy given to the NHL champion.

People had been saying there could never be another Gretzky. Now Mario Lemieux was already being talked about as the next great superstar. Then he went out and scored nearly 350 points in one season at Laval.

Mario was ready for the NHL.

ROOKIE SENSATION

The NHL draft is set up so that the team with the worst record in the league has the first pick of the amateur players. So Lemieux didn't have a choice as to where he would play. While he was scoring all those points for Laval, the Pittsburgh Penguins were struggling with the poorest record in the NHL.

In 1982-1983, the Penguins were 18-53-9. That means they won 18 games, lost 53 and tied 9. A year later they were 16-58-6. Because of their last-place finish in 1983-1984, the Penguins had the first choice in the draft. They wasted no time in naming Mario Lemieux their top choice and the number-one pick in the entire league.

Hockey salaries, as a rule, aren't as high as those given baseball, football, and basketball players. But Lemieux got a pretty good contract from the Penguins. He would be paid $350,000 for each of his first two seasons as a pro. And to make the pro life a bit easier for a teenager who would be far from home, the Penguins wanted Lemieux to live with a local family during his rookie year.

"That way, we were sure he was eating right and keeping decent hours," said Ed Johnston, the Penguins's general manager and a former NHL goalie. "We also felt it was important for him to have a home base to work from and people he could lean on."

It was a good idea. Lemieux was an 18-year-old boy who spoke almost no English. That could make being away from home difficult. He had taken a course in English while playing for Laval, but at Pittsburgh he found a better way to learn the language.

"I watched a lot of soap operas on television my first year," he explained.

Not knowing the language well made talking to reporters difficult.

It's time to go pro. A smiling Mario dons the jersey of the Pittsburgh Penguins for the first time after signing with the National Hockey League club in 1984. Standing with his soon-to-be-famous son is Jean-Guy Lemieux, Mario's father.

"There were times when I would answer 'yes,' 'no' or 'I think so' because I wasn't quite sure of the question," he said. Lemieux liked the city of Pittsburgh. He stayed at the home of Nancy and Tom Mathews. They had three sons all about his age and they got along well together. Lemieux had a strong family base while he got used to playing in the NHL. When he found his own place the next year, it was very close to the Mathews's home.

"It was like having another mother," Lemieux said of Nancy Mathews.

Even when he was starring with the Penguins, Mario would still play ball-hockey games with the Mathews boys in the street in front of their house.

There was a lot expected of Lemieux his rookie year. He was being asked to save the franchise. There were rumors the team might be sold or maybe moved to another city. There were too many empty seats at the Civic Arena. The fans had not been coming out to see the Penguins play.

But in Lemieux's rookie year there was a 46 percent jump in attendance from the year before. That was a big increase in one year, and the reason was the kid wearing number 66. But he didn't need a number to be noticed on the ice. His long, gliding stride was easy to spot and so was his size. At 6 feet 4 inches (193 centimeters) tall and two hundred pounds (74.6 kilograms), he looked more like a basketball player than a hockey player. But as soon as he took to the ice, there was no doubt about his ability.

In fact, when big guys like Lemieux play hockey, most are put on

A jubilant Mario celebrates his first National Hockey League goal. It came against the Boston Bruins at the outset of the 1984-1985 season. There would be many more moments like this for the big center, who would soon be called an all-time great.

defense. As a rule, the big players aren't fast, but they can throw their weight around. Lemieux was different. He had the quickness of a smaller player and could skate and stickhandle better than most of them. With a great shot and the ability to pass, he was a natural center.

"Mario is a very deceptive skater," said Ron Sutter of Philadelphia. "He doesn't look quick. But believe me, when he wants to go, he goes."

Lemieux was also beginning to score. Around the net, he used his size and strength. Defensemen couldn't move him out of the "slot." He also used his passing skills to set up his teammates. Within a very short time he became the leader of the Penguins's attack.

With Lemieux in the lineup the Penguins were better than they had been

As a rookie, Mario found his NHL legs quickly. His size and strength allowed him to adapt to the rough style of the pro game, and his great scoring ability would allow him to tally an even 100 points in his first season.

the last two years. But more good players were still needed. The difference was that the team now had a building block.

Lemieux was even better during the second half of the season. He was learning to cope with the pro game and scoring even more. When the season ended, the Penguins had a 24-51-5 record. But they were still last in the division—only one team in the league had a poorer record.

Lemieux ended the season with 43 goals and 57 assists for 100 points. Only two rookies in NHL history had ever scored more. Better yet, he had done it despite playing on a very poor team. To no one's surprise, Lemieux was named the NHL's Rookie of the Year for the 1984-1985 season.

FORCE ON THE ICE

During the next two seasons, Lemieux filled out to 210 pounds (78.33 kilograms), making him one of the biggest and strongest centers in the league. Beginning with the first half of the 1985-1986 season he was a real force on the ice.

Then came the annual NHL All-Star Game. Lemieux was brilliant. He led his team to a 6-4 victory and was named the game's Most Valuable Player.

"Winning the All-Star game MVP really made him feel he belonged," said Penguins general manager Eddie Johnston. "From then on, he took off."

Lemieux was quickly becoming an outstanding two-way player. That meant he did an excellent job on defense as well as offense. He learned to use his size to throw hard body checks, and also to work his way close to the net for a shot.

"Mario's strength gives his game a whole different dimension," said Philadelphia Flyers coach Mike Keenan. "He's learned how to beat you with his size. That's why he's so effective around the net."

His size and long arms also made it very hard for his opponents to take the puck from him. If a defenseman went right at him, Lemieux could usually stickhandle around him while still controlling the puck. He would put the puck out ahead of him, making a defenseman think he could take it. Once the defenseman made his move, Lemieux would reach out with his long arms and pull the puck back. Then, with a quick move, he would skate around the defender to either the inside or outside.

But the best part was that his great play had the Penguins winning. After 59 games, the team had a 28-25-6 record and was battling the New York Islanders for third place in the Patrick Division.

Lemieux had 38 goals and 72 assists by then, good for 110 points. That put him second to Gretzky in the NHL scoring race. The Great One was still well in front with 164 points, but Lemieux was closing the gap.

The Pens slumped a bit toward the end of the season. They finished with a 34-38-8 record and just missed getting into the playoffs. Lemieux finished his second year with 48 goals and 93 assists for 141 points, while Gretzky again led the league with 52 goals and a record 163 assists. That gave him a new scoring mark of 215 points.

During the off-season, the Penguins rewarded Lemieux with a new contract for $2.75 million over five years. At the time, it was the second-best contract in the league. The only player with a better one was Wayne Gretzky.

One of Lemieux's agents, Bob Perno, was amazed at how calm the youngster was.

"I was really nervous when we were ready to sign his new contract," Perno said. "So was his dad. While we were sitting in the Penguins's offices, Mario said, 'Let's play Intellivision Football.' So we played and he was more interested in beating me at that game than in signing a huge contract."

There was always excitement when Mario and Wayne Gretzky were on the ice together. In the eyes of many, they are the two greatest scorers in NHL history. Mario didn't hesitate to play tough against the Great One, even in their first meeting shown here. The game was played in Pittsburgh during Mario's rookie year, when Gretzky was still a member of the Edmonton Oilers.

In 1986-1987, more and more people were comparing him to Gretzky. Lemieux was asked about the Great One constantly. Yet he always kept a cool head.

"No, I'm not at the same level as Gretzky yet," he said before the mid-season All-Star game. "I'm just excited to be here because it's the best against the best. It will be fun."

What bothered Lemieux the most about the 1986-1987 season was missing 17 games because of injury. He wasn't hurt very often and hated to miss any games. He still finished with 54 goals and 53 assists for 107 points. Worse yet, the Penguins again failed to make the playoffs. The team ended the season at 30-38-12. There were just not enough good players.

Then, before the start of the 1987-1988 season, Lemieux joined an all-star team playing for Canada in a world-wide tournament. It was called the Canada Cup and had nothing to do with the NHL season. For the first time, though, Lemieux played alongside Wayne Gretzky. People say this tournament changed Mario Lemieux forever.

SCORING CHAMP

Much of the credit for the change in Lemieux belongs to Gretzky. Skating with the Great One, Lemieux saw something firsthand.

"Every shift, every time we were on the ice, Wayne tried to do the impossible," Lemieux said.

He meant that Gretzky never let up. He always worked very hard and looked for new ways to beat his opponents. With Gretzky setting him up,

Lemieux led all scorers as Canada won the tournament. He had 11 goals, and 9 were set up by passes from Gretzky. But it was watching Gretzky's work ethic that inspired Lemieux.

"Playing alongside Wayne gave me a lot of confidence in myself," Mario said. "And I brought it back to Pittsburgh."

His confidence showed on the ice. During the first half of the season Lemieux jumped out into the scoring lead. Gretzky had won every NHL scoring title since 1979. Now Lemieux was ahead of him. And he was showing no sign of slowing down.

On February 9, 1988, Lemieux joined all the other top players in St. Louis for the yearly All-Star game. Some say it was the game in which Mario Lemieux really showed the hockey world how far he had come. Each time the red light went on for his team (the signal for a goal scored), Lemieux had a hand in it.

At the end of regulation time Lemieux already had two goals and three assists. But the score was tied at 5-5, so the game went into sudden-death overtime. The first team that scored would win. Again the puck came to Lemieux. He skated in on goal, faked out one defenseman, then whistled a quick wrist shot past the goaltender for the winning score. He was everyone's pick for Most Valuable Player.

Although just 22 years old, Lemieux was again being compared to the Great Gretzky.

"Wayne has proved it every year, year after year," said former NHL star Bobby Clarke. "Mario has mountains to climb before he can be called as good as Wayne."

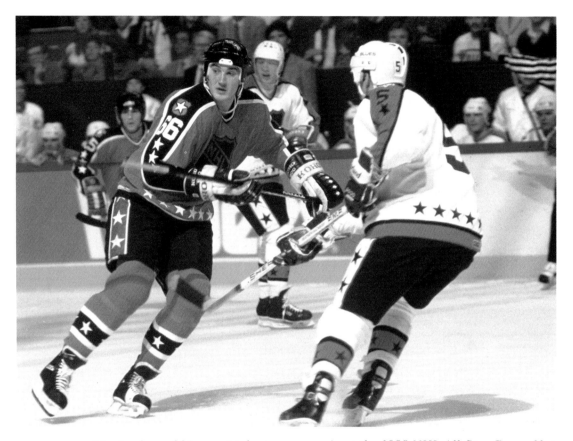

Mario showed his great talents once again at the 1988 NHL All-Star Game. Not only did he score two goals and add three assists in regulation play, but it was his goal in sudden-death overtime that gave his team a 6-5 victory. Needless to say, Mario was named the game's Most Valuable Player.

He was climbing fast. Teammate Randy Cunnyworth said, "He's 22, I'm 26, and a lot of times I find myself looking up to him."

When the 1987-1988 season ended, Lemieux had won his first NHL scoring title. He had a league-best 70 goals. He also had 98 assists for 168 points. Gretzky finished second with 40 goals and 109 assists for 149 points.

Once again, however, the Penguins just missed making the playoffs. The team finished with a 36-35-9 record. It wasn't until the last day of the season that they lost the final playoff spot. Lemieux and his teammates were all disappointed.

After the season, Lemieux was named the winner of the Hart Trophy, given to the league's Most Valuable Player. Gretzky had won the prize eight straight years until Lemieux got it. He also won the Lester Pearson Award, voted on by all the NHL players.

But Lemieux wanted more than awards for his own play. He wanted to play on a winning team. With Gretzky leading the way, the Edmonton Oilers had won four Stanley Cups (championships) in the past five years. Lemieux had similar hopes for the Penguins.

The Penguins as a team were beginning to get better players in 1987-1988. In November of 1987 the Pens made a trade with Edmonton. They got defenseman Paul Coffey, one of the best in the league. Two years earlier he had set a record for defensemen by scoring 48 goals. He was also a two-time winner of the Norris Trophy, given to the best defenseman in the league.

Young center Rob Brown was a rookie in 1987-1988. That year he scored 24 goals in just 51 games and looked like a coming star. The club would also make a trade with Buffalo in early November 1988, for goal-

Mario was the toast of the town after a brilliant 1987-1988 season. He added to his collection of hardware when he won the Hart Trophy as the NHL's Most Valuable Player, as well as the Art Ross Trophy for winning the league scoring title. He had 70 goals and 98 assists for 168 points.

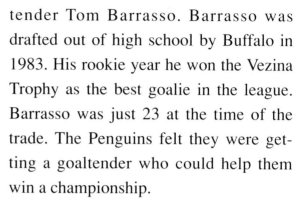

tender Tom Barrasso. Barrasso was drafted out of high school by Buffalo in 1983. His rookie year he won the Vezina Trophy as the best goalie in the league. Barrasso was just 23 at the time of the trade. The Penguins felt they were getting a goaltender who could help them win a championship.

There were more good young players coming along in the system. Things were looking very good for the future. And at the beginning of the 1988-1989 season, Lemieux began scoring at a record pace. Some nights it seemed as if no one could stop him. And even better, the Penguins were winning.

By the time the Penguins had played 36 games, Lemieux already had 104

Mario is an outstanding skater who uses his strength and size to protect the puck. He is also tough to stop. Standing 6-foot-4 and weighing well over 200 pounds, Mario has often scored with two defensemen hanging over him.

points. Only Gretzky had ever reached 100 points in a season faster. Lemieux also had an 18-point lead over Gretzky in the scoring race. But the best news was that the Penguins were leading their division. The team had a 23-12-3 record and a four-point lead over the second place Rangers.

Most of the talk, however, was about Lemieux. His new coach, Gene Ubriaco, said he had the best puck-handling skills he had ever seen. "Once he gets behind you, he cannot be legally stopped," added the coach.

Teammate Randy Cunneyworth couldn't believe how strong Lemieux was. He recalled one game against the Vancouver Canucks. Cunneyworth said he sat on the bench watching Lemieux stickhandle through almost the whole team.

"They were literally falling at his feet, one after another," said Cunneyworth. "I froze that picture: three guys behind Mario on the ice, in a heap. I'll never forget it. He ended up behind the net and just reached around and stuffed the puck in. I was on the bench and just started laughing."

When the season ended, Lemieux was the talk of the league. He finished with 85 goals and 114 assists for a league-leading 199 points. He led the league in total goals and in power-play goals (31), and set a new NHL record with 13 shorthanded scores. He was the All-Star center for the year and again won the Lester Pearson Award as the players' choice MVP.

But this time he had help, especially from center Rob Brown, defenseman Paul Coffey, and center Dan Quinn. The team finished the year with a 40-33-7 record, good for second place in the Patrick Division. They were in the playoffs at last.

In the first round, the Penguins swept the New York Rangers in four

straight games. They did it with a solid team effort.

"Playing with Mario is a thrill," said Randy Cunneyworth. "But as good as he is, we know we have to do the job, too, or we won't win. He can't do it all by himself."

Then came the division finals against Philadelphia. The Penguins took a 3-2 lead in the best-of-seven series. But the Flyers bounced back to take the final two games, 6-2 and 4-1, to win it. The Penguins were out, but they had surprised a lot of people.

In the fifth game of the Philly series, Lemieux once again had an eight-point performance. He scored his first three goals in just 6 minutes and 55 seconds, and had a record four goals in one period. For the playoffs, he had 12

Even when he is taking a rest on the bench, Mario keeps his eyes on the game. He and his Penguins teammates follow the action closely, waiting for the word to leap over the boards onto the ice so they can get back into the flow of the game.

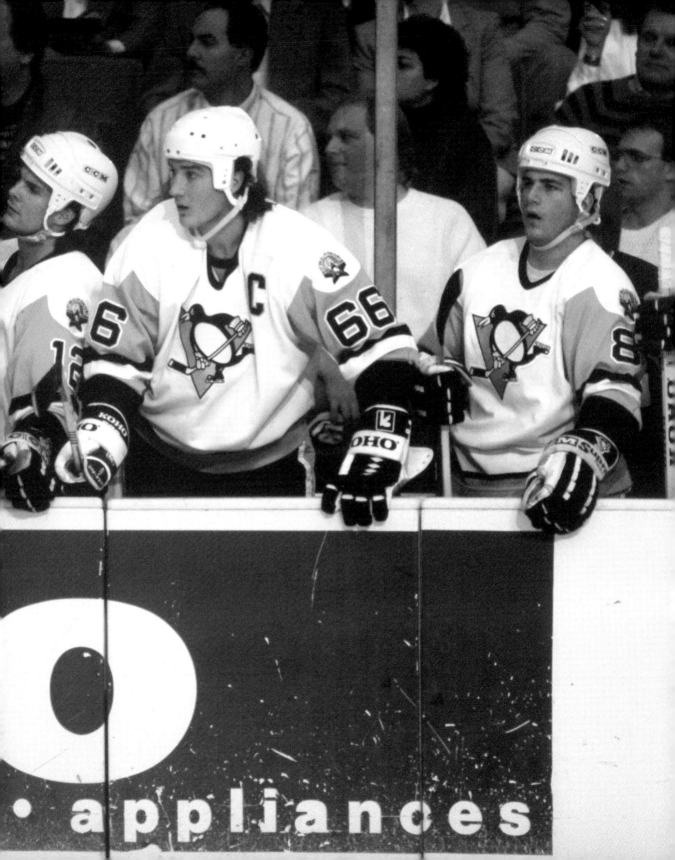

goals and 7 assists in 11 games. Shortly after it ended, he was named Player of the Year by the *Sporting News.*

A MAJOR SETBACK

The hockey world simply couldn't say enough good things about Mario Lemieux. His teammate, Rob Brown, again made the comparison with Wayne Gretzky.

"I grew up watching Gretzky for six years in Edmonton," he said, "and I never thought I'd see his equal as a player. Then I came to Pittsburgh."

Super Mario and the Great One were the two biggest stars in hockey. Gretzky was still considered the greatest team player ever, but Lemieux's size and individual skills were a combination no other player had.

People were also interested in what Lemieux did off the ice. When he wasn't playing hockey, his great passion was golf. He loved to be out on the fairways. He even talked about maybe becoming a golf pro when his hockey career was over. Some of his teammates and friends teased him about being a couch potato. Away from the ice Lemieux liked to sleep and watch television, they said.

His favorite TV show was "Cheers." He had a steady girlfriend and by this time spoke English very well. That didn't mean he liked to talk, though. Reporters often found his answers to their questions short and to the point.

Before the 1989-1990 season, Lemieux was rewarded with yet another new contract. It was for $10 million over five years, with another $3 million in bonuses.

Lemieux and his teammates wanted one thing now: the Stanley Cup. Their goal was to be champions. Many wanted to know if Super Mario thought he could score 100 goals in a season.

"It can be done," he said, "but only if you play on a strong team."

The Penguins had a bigger, stronger team at the beginning of the 1989-1990 season. But for some reason they got off to a bad start. After 17 games, the team was just 5-10-2 and in fifth place. Lemieux was second to Gretzky in scoring, 35-30, and in the eyes of many he was not playing as well as he had.

In November, he had some tests done by a doctor. The results showed he was okay.

"I'm not skating as well as last year," he admitted. "I've had no jump, no energy. It's the way I feel every day. I've been like this for almost a month."

Because the team was lagging, the pressure on Lemieux was building up.

"I know I have to go out there and get two, three, or four points almost every night," he said. "That's the only way I'm going to help the team win."

But as the season wore on, both Lemieux and the Penguins began coming alive. The new players were blending in with the old, giving the team a real "chemistry" for the first time. And after 56 games, the big guy was back on top in the scoring race. He had 43 goals and 77 assists for 120 points. Gretzky was next with 29-78-107. It looked like Lemieux was on his way to a third straight scoring title.

The Penguins were at 26-27-4, tied for second in the Patrick Division with the Rangers and New Jersey Devils. But there was only a 10-point difference between the first and last team in the division.

It was at this point in the season that the story first broke in the newspapers. It came as a surprise to everyone: Lemieux had been playing all year with a bad back. He had a herniated disk, and he told the press there was a good chance he would need surgery after the season. But now, suddenly, the pain was getting worse. The question was whether he could keep playing.

He tried it with a back brace. "We sometimes have to adjust the brace after a couple of shifts," he said. "But I want to keep playing. I think it's better for me to keep playing.

"I feel I can still go out and help the team, especially on the power play. Once I can't do that anymore, then we'll see about getting a little rest."

Two games later Lemieux just couldn't take the pain any more. It

It's never easy for an athlete to come back from a serious injury. Mario knew he would have to work hard to return to his old form following back surgery. Here he mugs for the cameras while riding a stationary bike in the training room at the Civic Arena. Once back, he led the Penguins to the Stanley Cup.

looked as if he would be out the remainder of the regular season. Without Super Mario, the team didn't have that little extra. They finished at 32-40-8 and in fifth place. No playoffs. Lemieux played one game at the end of the year and managed three more points. In 59 games he had 45 goals and 78 assists for 123 points. That was good enough for fourth place in scoring.

He was still facing surgery on his back—a scary prospect for a young player. A bad back can easily end a player's career.

THE STANLEY CUP

On July 11, 1990, Lemieux finally had the operation on his back. Three months later he was skating again. He hoped to be ready to play shortly after the start of the new season. Then there was another setback.

The doctors told him he had an infection in his back. He wouldn't be able to play for at least three months.

"Everybody has seen Mario in the shower, grimacing in pain, so we knew there was a chance he might not play for a while," said his teammate Phil Bourque.

So the team had to go on without Lemieux. They had a new coach in Bob Johnson and a number of new players, such as Mark Recchi and Kevin Stevens.

Even without Lemieux, the Penguins battled for the division lead for the first half of the season. Coach Johnson was a veteran hockey man who knew how to handle his players. It wasn't until the last third of the season that Lemieux was finally able to return.

Once he was back, the Penguins were even better. The team finished strong and won the Patrick Division with a 41-33-6 record. Lemieux played the final 26 games and scored 19 goals with 26 assists for 45 points. He was just about back to his old self.

After beating the New Jersey Devils in the first round of the playoffs, the Penguins went up against the Washington Capitals in the Patrick Division finals. With the series tied at one game each, the Penguins turned it on. Goalie Barrasso was brilliant. The Pens won the last three games, 3-1, 3-1 and 4-1 to take the series.

Next came the conference finals against Boston. The Bruins won the first two games. But then Lemieux and Barrasso led a comeback. Pittsburgh took the series and moved on to the Stanley Cup finals. To win it, they would have to beat the Minnesota North Stars. The North Stars hadn't been that good during the regular season, but they caught fire in the playoffs to reach the final round.

The North Stars won the first game, 5-4. Then, with the Penguins holding a 2-1 lead in game two, Lemieux scored a goal that lifted the team.

He took a pass from Phil Bourque and skated into North Star ice. From there, he headed straight at defenseman Shawn Chambers. At the

While Mario was recovering from back surgery, his teammates had to play extra hard. One of the Pittsburgh stars who helped to keep the team winning was high-scoring defenseman Paul Coffey. Coffey had come to the Penguins in 1987-1988 after playing alongside Wayne Gretzky at Edmonton. Once in Pittsburgh, he continued his all-star caliber of play.

last second, he faked outside, then cut back inside. From there he backhand-
ed the puck between Chambers's legs, skated around him and picked it up
again. Now he came in on goalie Jon Casey.

Lemieux then switched the puck to his backhand and faked Casey right
out of the net. The fake took him to his knees, but he still slid the puck into
the open net. It was a brilliant effort. The Pens won the game, 4-1. Kevin
Stevens, who had scored twice in the game, knew how well Lemieux was
playing.

"I love to see it," Stevens said. "People don't know how bad his injury
was. He had to lie in bed for seven or eight weeks and now he's come back
like this. He's got guys on him all night and he's getting hit all the time."

Then before game three there was a minor setback. Lemieux had bad
back pains before the game and couldn't play. The doctor said it was muscle
spasms and that he would probably be all right for the next game. Without
him, the Penguins lost the third game, 3-1.

Up to that point, Mario was leading the playoffs in scoring. He had 13
goals and 35 points. He had also scored a point in 15 straight games and a
goal in 7 straight. Sure enough, he was back on the ice for game four.

He played well as the Pens scored three times in less than three minutes
to open up a big lead. They won the game, 5-3. Then, in game five, Lemieux
was again outstanding. He scored the first goal, set up the third and was

Hockey is always an all-out, play-hard sport. Players
returning from injuries don't have it any easier.
Mario knew he would have to be ready to hit and be hit
despite his bad back. Here he looks up ice after
making a pass against the Edmonton Oilers.

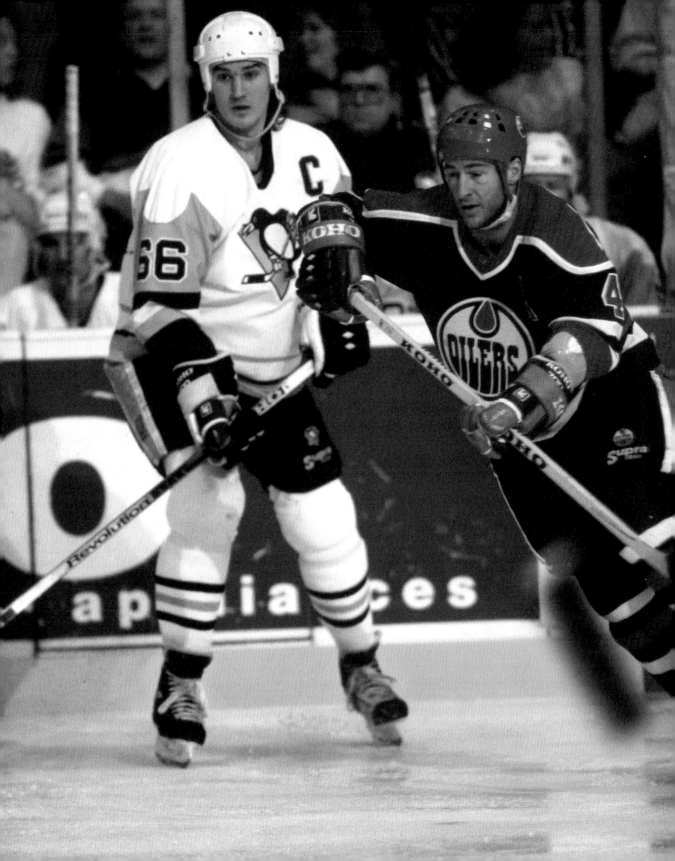

checking hard all over the ice. Pittsburgh won it, 6-4. The Penguins had a 3-2 lead and were a win away from the championship.

In game six, the Pens came out flying once again. Goals by Ulf Samuelsson, Joey Mullen, and Lemieux made it 3-0 in the first period. From

It's every hockey player's dream to hold the Stanley Cup, the trophy given to the NHL champion every year. When the Penguins won the Cup in 1991, the city of Pittsburgh went wild, and all the players wanted a chance to pose with the ancient and revered trophy. Here Mario and teammate Paul Coffey (right) take turns hoisting the Cup.

there, the Penguins coasted to an 8-0 victory. They were the Stanley Cup champions!

After the game ended, Lemieux skated around the ice surrounded by his teammates. He held the Stanley Cup high over his head. This is a longstanding hockey tradition.

"This is the ultimate dream," Lemieux said afterward. "There are guys who play 10 to 15 years in the league and never even get a chance to be in the finals."

Super Mario had scored 44 points in the playoffs and was named the winner of the Conn Smythe Trophy as the Most Valuable Player. Goalie Barrasso and the rest of the team had given him great support. He no longer had to be a one-man gang. Without Lemieux, the Pens had become a good hockey team. With him, they showed they could be special. Maybe goalie Barrasso put it best. "There wasn't going to be hockey in Pittsburgh anymore if not for Mario," he said. "And we wouldn't have won the Cup without him."

As for Lemieux, he gave a lot of credit to Coach Johnson. "Nobody thought we could win the Cup," Mario said, "but Bob came here and was so positive. He made us believe anything was possible. He convinced us we could win the Stanley Cup."

Mario Lemieux has become a true hero in Pittsburgh. He has made the city his year-round home. When not playing hockey, Lemieux has often played in charity golf tournaments. Golf has remained a second love. He has also worked with the Pittsburgh Cancer Institute and a number of other local charities.

At the outset of the 1991-1992 season Super Mario was again playing well. Although his back still gave him some trouble, he was among the league leaders in scoring by December. Back problems, however, can come at any time. Hockey fans only hope Lemieux will stay healthy and have a long career.

It seems as if the only thing that can stop Mario Lemieux is his back. Although he recovered from surgery to lead the Penguins to the Stanley Cup, Mario still has periods when back pain keeps him out of the lineup.

MARIO LEMIEUX: HIGHLIGHTS

1965	Born on October 5 in Montreal, Canada.
1981	Joins the Laval junior hockey club in Quebec, Canada.
1982	Compiles a 30/66/96 (goals/assists/total) record.
1983	Compiles an 84/100/184 record.
1984	Compiles a 133/149/282 record. Signs with NHL Pittsburgh Penguins.
1985	Compiles a 43/57/100 record as a rookie. Named NHL Rookie of the Year.
1986	Named NHL All-Star Game's MVP. Compiles a 48/93/141 record.
1987	Compiles a 54/53/107 record in spite of injuries.
1988	Compiles a 70/98/168 record. Wins the NHL scoring title with a league-best 70 goals. Wins the Hart Trophy as NHL's MVP. Wins the Lester Pearson Award.
1989	Compiles an 85/114/199 record. Wins the Lester Pearson Award. Named NHL All-Star center. Named Player of the Year by the *Sporting News*.
1990	Compiles a 45/78/123 record with back injury.
1991	Compiles a 19/26/45 record in spite of injuries. Penguins win the Stanley Cup. Wins the Conn Smythe Trophy as MVP.
1992	Penguins win the Stanley Cup. Leads NHL in scoring in regular season. Wins the Conn Smythe trophy as MVP.

FIND OUT MORE

Aaseng, Nathan. *Hockey's Fearless Goalies*. Minneapolis, MN: Lerner, 1984.

_____, *Hockey's Super Scorers*. Minneapolis, MN: Lerner, 1984.

Bianchi, J. *Champions of Hockey*. Ontario: Firefly Books, 1989.

Gutman, Bill. *Go For It: Ice Hockey*. Lakeville, CT: Grey Castle Press, 1989.

Maclean, Norman. *Hockey Basics*. New York: Prentice Hall, 1983.

Rennie, Ross. *Pittsburgh Penguins*. Mankato, MN: Creative Education, 1990.

INDEX